D1126229

CHLOE KIM

by Elizabeth Raum

AMICUS HIGH INTEREST • AMICUS INK

Amicus High Interest and Amicus Ink are imprints of Amicus
P.O. Box 1329, Mankato, MN 56002
www.amicuspublishing.us

Library of Congress Cataloging-in-Publication Data
Names: Raum, Elizabeth, author.
Title: Chloe Kim / by Elizabeth Raum.
Description: Mankato, Minnesota : Amicus, 2018. | Series: Amicus High
    Interest. Pro Sports Biographies | Includes index. | Audience: K to Grade 3.
Identifiers: LCCN 2016058344 (print) | LCCN 2017004856 (ebook) ISBN
    9781681511344 (library binding) | ISBN 9781681521657 (pbk.) | ISBN
    9781681512242 (ebook)
Subjects: LCSH: Kim, Chloe, 2000- | Women snowboarders--United
    States--Biography--Juvenile literature. | Snowboarders--United States--
    Biography--Juvenile literature.
Classification: LCC GV857.S57 K557 2018 (print) | LCC GV857.S57 (ebook) |
    DDC 796.939092 [B] --dc23
LC record available at https://lccn.loc.gov/2016058344

Photo Credits: Gian Ehrenzeller/Keystone/Associated Press cover;
VasutinSergey/Shutterstock background pattern; Doug Pensinger/Getty
Images 2; Jon Buckle/IOC/Getty Images 4–5, 22; Gabe L'Heureux/Getty
Images 7; Eric Lars Bakke/ESPN Images 8–9; Arnt Folvik/YIS/IOC/
Getty Images 10–11; Vegard Wivestad Grot/NTB Scanpix/AP
12–13; Tom Pennington/Getty Images 14–15, 20–21;
U.S. Snowboarding/Smugmug 16; Sipa USA/AP 19

Editor: Wendy Dieker
Designer: Aubrey Harper
Photo Researcher: Holly Young

Printed in the United States of America

HC 10 9 8 7 6 5 4 3 2 1
PB 10 9 8 7 6 5 4 3 2 1

TABLE OF CONTENTS

SNOWBOARD STAR

Chloe Kim slides down one side of the **halfpipe**. She flies up the other side. She spins and flips in the air. The crowd goes wild. This young snowboarder is a winner.

STARTING OUT

Chloe Kim was born in California. She was four when she started snowboarding. She went **pro** when she was only 13. It wasn't long before she was winning halfpipe competitions.

YOUNG PRO

Kim was the youngest snowboarder on the pro team in 2013. But she still won halfpipe medals. She won a silver medal at her first **X Games (XG)** in 2014.

GOLD MEDALS

Kim then won the XG gold in 2015 and 2016. She became the youngest XG athlete to win two gold medals. In 2016, Kim won two gold medals in the Youth Olympic Games. She won the halfpipe and **slopestyle** events.

RIDING SWITCH

Kim rides best with her right foot forward. Her coach made her learn to **ride switch**. She had to put her left foot forward. It was hard. She practiced. Now it's easy.

Kim says riding switch is like running backwards.

1080

Riding switch helps Kim do hard tricks. In 2015, she landed her first **1080**. It is a tough trick. She soars high above the pipe. Then she spins around three times and lands. Few riders can do it.

1080 X 2

Kim wanted to do something even harder. She did two 1080s in a row. She did it at the U.S. Snowboarding Grand Prix in 2016. She was the first woman to land two in a row.

Kim's back-to-back 1080s earned her a perfect score of 100. She was the first woman to get that score.

TEEN STAR

Kim is still a teenager. But people look up to her. *Teen Vogue* put her on its "21 under 21" list. These are girls under the age of 21 who are changing the world.

19

LOOKING AHEAD

In 2016, Kim was ranked the best female halfpipe snowboarder in the world. She was only 16 years old. Chloe Kim has many more years of snowboarding ahead of her.

JUST THE FACTS

Born: April 23, 2000

Hometown: La Palma, California

Joined the pros: 2013

Discipline: Halfpipe

Stats: www.worldsnowboardtour.com/riders/chloe-kim/

Accomplishments:

- Youngest rider to become a member of U.S. Snowboarding Pro halfpipe team

- XG Aspen gold medals: 2015, 2016

- World Snowboard Tour leader: 2015, 2016

- FIS World Cup halfpipe title winner: 2017

- First woman to land back-to-back 1080s

- First woman to earn a perfect 100 score

- Ranked #1 female halfpipe rider in the world: 2016

WORDS TO KNOW

1080 – a snowboard trick where the rider spins three times in the air before landing

halfpipe – a U-shaped ramp used in snowboarding to do tricks

pro – short for professional; a person who is paid to compete in a sport.

riding switch – to ride the snowboard with the opposite foot forward of how you normally ride. For example, if you are right-footed, you put your left forward.

slopestyle – a downhill snowboard event that involves sliding on rails, jumping, and doing tricks

X Games (XG) – an extreme sports contest held by the ESPN sports network

LEARN MORE

Books

Waxman, Laura Hamilton. *Snowboarding*. Winter Olympic Sports. Mankato, Minn.: Amicus, 2018.

Hamilton, John. *Snowboarding*. Action Sports. Minneapolis, Minn.: ABDO, 2015.

Mason, Paul. *Snowboarding*. Winter Sports. Chicago, Ill.: Raintree, 2014.

Websites

Olympic Snowboarding | Winter Olympic Sport
https://www.olympic.org/snowboard

Chloe Kim | U.S. Snowboarding
http://ussnowboarding.com/athletes/chloe-kim

INDEX